TIME WELL SPENT

Lula Latigue

ISBN 979-8-89130-178-8 (paperback)
ISBN 979-8-89130-179-5 (digital)

Copyright © 2024 by Lula Latigue

All rights reserved. No part of this publication may be reproduced, distributed, or transmitted in any form or by any means, including photocopying, recording, or other electronic or mechanical methods without the prior written permission of the publisher. For permission requests, solicit the publisher via the address below.

Christian Faith Publishing
832 Park Avenue
Meadville, PA 16335
www.christianfaithpublishing.com

Printed in the United States of America

TIME WELL SPENT

I graduated from Joseph Celestine High School in 1966. I was privileged to have the best teachers on staff. They were all great. One stood out—Mrs. R. She took me under her wing when our mom passed away. It's God's grace we made it without abuse from many. Our dad kept us together in our home. Many wanted this one, that one, but he said, "No, they all staying here and going to school and will finish. Their mom said they have to stay and finish school."

I played basketball, tennis, baseball (as pitcher), and flag football, joined the band, played the flute, did skits, and was president of our class for four years. I still do not remember what that was about. I graduated salutatorian. If there were scholarships for basketball, I was sure I would have received one. I was a twenty-five pointer per game or less at times.

We started off with twenty-one students at senior year. We were down to five. Some students had to help parents harvest sharecrop or dropped out. I believe everyone did well, regardless of their circumstances.

I received a scholarship and went to Dallas Business Institute. I did not finish. We found a dead body under the building, and I asked to come home. And a ticket was sent. I returned home to Vidrine. I applied at my alma mater, was hired, and life began.

Monsanto was born in 1967.

Chauncy was born in 1969.

I never thought to abort. I wanted my children and loved them in my womb. I would read the Bible daily to them as I carried them in my womb. I was not sick. I carried well and delivered Monsanto in the hospital and Chauncy at home.

Then I met my husband when Monsanto was two years old and Chauncy was nine months old. He accepted my children as his. We discussed having one more. If it happened, okay, if not, we were okay.

We set up a house and worked at our jobs, living as a family.

One day, after getting home, my live-in man asked me to marry him. "Lady, will you marry me, make me the happiest man on earth?"

I said, "Yes, I will, mister."

I ended up being a great daughter-in-law. I respected his parents and was cordial to the extended family.

3

I stayed in the hospital with my mother-in-law as my husband stayed with the children. We had Donnie by then and had lost two boys. My mother-in-law died in my arms at the hospital in Alexandria. How do you call and report that the rest is a blur? I watched as my husband changed a little.

I believe the Bible to be the inspired Word of God, the infallible Word of God.

All scripture is given by inspiration of God, and is profitable for doctrine, for reproof, for correction, for instruction in righteousness.

> And without controversy great is the mystery of godliness: God was manifest in the flesh, justified in the Spirit, seen of angels, preached unto the Gentiles, believed on in the world, received up into glory. (1 Timothy 3:16 KJV)

The Bible is the only God-given authority that man possesses; therefore, all doctrine, faith, hope, and all instructions for the church must be based upon and harmonized with the Bible. It gives a true history of the creation of the heavens and the earth and of all mankind and contains a correct prophecy of the ages to come regarding the heavens and the earth and the destiny of man.

There is not salvation outside of that which is contained within the pages of King James Version. The interpretation is not private when read. The understanding and revelation comes from God, his Spirit, to the person reading it.

I do not debate the Word of God. I do not know everything or understand everything I read in the Bible.

I have read the Bible from cover to maps four times in my life before and after salvation. I know enough to remain saved, sanctified, and prayer can get through to my sovereign God (1 John 2:27).

"No prophecy of the scripture is of any private interpretation. For the prophecy came not in old time by the will of man, but Holy men of God spake as they were moved by the Holy Ghost" (2 Peter 1:20–21).

THE ONE TRUE GOD

I believe in the one ever-living eternal God—infinite in power, holy in nature, attributes and purpose and possessing absolute, indivisible deity.

The Scripture does more than attempt to prove the existence of God; it asserts, assumes, and declares that the knowledge of God is universal.

This one true God has revealed himself as Father, through his son, in redemptions, and as the Holy Spirit, by emanation (1 Corinthians 8:6, Ephesians 4:6, 2 Corinthians 5:19, Joel 2:28).

The knowledge of God is universal (Romans 1:9, 21, 28, 32 and 2:15).

God is invisible, incorporeal, without parts, without body, and free from all limitations.

He is spirit (John 4:24), and a spirit hath no flesh and bones (Luke 24:39).

I believe there is one God.

Father is God.

Son is God.

Holy Ghost is God.

Some say Holy Spirit, when he shows up, you will know!

The first of all commandments is "Hear, O Israel: The Lord our God is one God" (Deuteronomy 6:4). "And Jesus answered him, The first of all commandments is, Hear; O Israel; The Lord our God is one God" (Mark 12:29).

Father:

> Thus saith the Lord the King of Israel, and his redeemer the Lord of hosts; I am the first,

and I am the last; and beside me there is no God. (Isaiah 44:6)

Ye are my witnesses, saith the Lord, and my servant whom I have chosen: that ye may know and believe me, and understand that I am he: before me there was no God formed, neither shall there be after me. (Isaiah 43:10)

Son:

Jesus is the Son of God according to the flesh (Romans 1:3) and the very God himself according to the Spirit (Matthew 1:23).

The Jehovah of the Old Testament took upon himself the form of man and, as the Son of man, was born of the Virgin Mary.

As Paul says in 1 Timothy 3:16, "And without controversy great is the mystery of Godliness: God was manifested in the flesh, justified in the Spirit, seen of angels, preached unto the Gentiles, believed on in the world, received up into Glory."

The right hand of power is the glory of God (Mark 14:62).

I believe that in him, Jesus dwells all the fullness of the Godhead bodily (Colossians 2:9).

Therefore, Jesus in his humanity was man and in his deity was and is God (Colossians 1:19).

His flesh was the lamb or the sacrifice of God.

He is the only mediator between God and man (1 Timothy 2:5).

Holy Ghost:

> The Holy Ghost is not the third person in the godhead but the manifestation of the Spirit of God (the creator) and the resurrected Christ, as the comforter, sustainer, and keeper (John 14:16–20).

So there are not three Gods but three manifestation of the one God (Romans 8:11).

These three are one (1 John 5:7).

In the beginning, God created man innocent, pure, and holy, but through the sin of disobedience, Adam and Eve, the first of human race, fell from their holy state, and God banished them from Eden (Genesis 1:27, Romans 3:23).

SIN

Sin is the transgression of the law or commandments of God 1 John 3:4, the guilt of which has fallen upon all men from the sin of Adam until this present time, the wages and results of which culminate in eternal death

Romans 6:23, Rev. 20:14, 15 to all those who refuse to accept salvation as set forth in the Word of God.

Pardon and forgiveness of sins is obtained by genuine repentance.

Forgiveness of sin is obtained by repentance—a confessing to God and asking for forgiveness and forsaking sin.

We are justified by *faith* in the Lord Jesus Christ (Romans 5:1).

John the Baptist preached repentance, Jesus proclaimed repentance, and the apostles emphasized it to both Jews and Gentiles (Acts 2:38, 11:18, 17:30).

"And that repentance and remission of sins should be preached in His name among all nations, beginning at Jerusalem" (Luke 24:47).

Water baptism is an essential part of New Testament salvation, and water baptism is not just an outward form of an inward cleansing. It is an essential part of the New Testament salvation. It is being fully immersed in water after repenting to God for sins. We sin against God and God only.

"Against thee, thee only, have I sinned and done this evil in thy sight: thou mighest be justified when thou speaketh, and be clear when thou judgest" (Psalm 51:4).

Acts 2:38, Acts 8:16, Acts 10:48, Acts 19:5, and Matthew 28:19.

Water baptism can be administered by immersion (Colossians 2:12).

Jesus mentioned being born of the water (John 3:5).

Water baptism removes sin and leaves it in a water grave, never to be remembered again by God.

Jesus came up out of the water (Mark 1:10).

Philip and the eunuch went down into the water and came up out of the water (Acts 8:38–39).

He that believers and is baptized shall be saved (Acts 2:47).

Father, Son, Holy Ghost are not names but titles held by God. Jesus is his name.

Jesus's last commandment to his disciples was "Go ye therefore and teach all nations baptizing them in the *name* of the Father Son Holy Ghost" (Matthew 28:19). We hear the angel announce, "She shall bring forth a Son and thou shalt call His *name Jesus*, for he shall save his people from their sins" (Matthew 1:21).

There is no other name under heaven, given among men, whereby we must be saved (Acts 4:12).

Baptism of the Holy Ghost

The baptism of the Holy Ghost is the birth of the Spirit (John 3:5)—that's spiritual baptism. It is evident by speaking in another tongue, other than your tongue you speak in, as the Spirit gives utterance.

No one can teach you how to speak in another tongue—it is given by God spiritually and supernaturally.

It was prophesied by Joel 2:28–29 and Isaiah 28:11, foretold by John the Baptist (Matthew 3:11), purchased by the blood of Jesus, and promised by him to the disciples (John 14:26, 15:26) and first outpoured on the day of Pentecost upon the Jews (Acts 2:1–4) then the Samaritans (Acts 8:17) and upon the Gentiles (Acts 10:44–46, 19:66).

And the promise is unto you and to your children and to all that are far off, even as many as the Lord our God shall call (Acts 2:30, Romans 8:9).

I was filled with the Holy Ghost and fire in my home at the foot of my bed.

I was supposed to meet people of the congregation at the civic center, to pass out pamphlets on the grounds. I never made it there.

My day started as usual. I prayed. My children were not home. I did not write where they were, but my husband was in the neighborhood, at our friend's home. Our home was clean. The food was cooked. I would get to the door to leave, and I would forget something, then the phone rang. The phone was in our bedroom.

I opened the door to our bedroom, picked up the phone, answered it. It was Monsanto. She said "Mommy, my head hurts so bad."

I said, "Let me pray for you."

We prayed. When I said, "In Jesus's name," she said, "I feel better."

I said, "Okay, lovie, talk later. I have to get to the civic center. Bye," as I put the receiver on the base and raised my hands to praise God. The ceiling to our bedroom opened up. I saw the heavens descending. The sky opened up. A huge silver nail was coming straight at me through the sky through the open ceiling. The nail entered my belly. "He that believe that on me, as the scripture hath said, out of his belly shall flow rivers of living water" (John 7:38).

The presence of God was so profound in our room. All kinds of tongues were coming out of my mouth. It was a glorious day. It was around 11:00 a.m. By the time I came to myself, it was after 3:00 p.m. During that time, my husband came home while God was filling me and giving gifts from him. How did I know? I saw my husband through the wall, and he was trying to open the bedroom door, but the door would not open. Instead, he was thrown backward. His body hit the wall, and his hands went up. Tears were falling from his face. God was still pouring in me until the wall came back in place, and I could not see him anymore. I was enjoying my God. I have been speaking in my own prayer language ever since that day.

When I finally came out of our room, he was nowhere to be found.

I told him that night what happened. He said, "That's good. I could not get inside at all."

God will not share his glory with anyone.

Tongues

Tongues have two classifications:

1. Speaking in other tongues as the Spirit gives utterance.
2. The gift of tongues as mentioned in 1 Corinthians.

Speaking in other tongues as the Spirit of God gives utterance is manifestation God has given, as a definite, indisputable, supernatural witness or sign of the baptism of the Holy Ghost. It was prophesied by the Prophet Isaiah as the "the rest and the refreshing" (Isaiah 28:11–12).

It was foretold by Jesus as a sign that would follow every believer of the gospel (Mark 16:16–17) and poured first upon the Jews at Pentecost, then the Gentiles at Caesarea, thus fulfilling the prophecy (Joel 2:38–29, Acts 2:15–18).

The gift of tongues or unknown tongues mentioned by Paul in 1 Corinthians 12:1, 10 and concerning which he gives revelations in 1 Corinthians 14:4 is the gift given by God. God can use any believer to utter his message and interpret the message to be used to edifying the congregation of sinners and believers (1 Corinthians 14:4), except when there is an interpreter present (1 Corinthians 14:27–28).

The gifts flow. There is a distant sound to tongues and interpretation. I was taught prophecy flows. I witness that many times sitting in a 3,000-seat building in Lake Charles, Louisiana, for fifteen years and in Abbeville, Louisiana, in full capacity of about 400 for twenty-three years.

"For I pray in an unknown tongue my spirit prayeth. But my understanding is unfruitful. The gift can be misused" (1 Corinthians 14:23–28).

Paul wrote "forbid not to speak with tongues" (1 Corinthians 14:39), and "I thank you my God I speak with tongues more than ye all" (1 Corinthians 14:18). Who dares to teach or preach to the contrary?

Holiness

After we are saved from sin, We are commanded to "Go and sin no more" (John 8:11).

We are commanded to live soberly, righteously, and godly in this present world (Titus 2:12) and warned that without holiness, no man shall see the Lord (Hebrews 12).

We must present ourselves holy unto the Lord (Romans 12:1), Cleanse ourselves from all filthiness of the flesh and spirit (2 Corinthians 7:1), and separate ourselves from all worldliness (James 4:4).

No man can do this by his own power, but he shall receive power after that the Holy Ghost has come upon you (Acts 1:8, Matthew 5:48).

Some put a way of dressing, wear no makeup, wear long dresses and skirts, and cover their armpits. "A spirit of Jezebel comes with you that if you apply lipstick," I was told, "and God is not pleased."

I believe that when your spiritual man conquers your flesh, then you change and stuff starts falling off and your apparel changes to fit your inner man. A self-righteous spirit comes with that when you try and tell someone not to dress a certain way.

Some do not know another way but try to get salvation started, and God will do the rest.

Leave people alone. It takes time for some to find the holiness path.

Come as you are to the Lord with your sin and repent and turn from your wicked ways and do not partake of the worldly ways. Old things are passed away. Behold, all things become new.

I chose not to wear makeup or lipstick. I believe I am fearfully and wonderfully made and do not need a mask to face the world or saints. I wear dresses and skirts and cover my body because I choose to do so. Every human being, male or female, is fearfully and wonderfully made. You have to know and like yourself to accept how you are.

The spiritual man conquers the flesh, and you get help from God to be able to reach that point in your everyday life. I have no problem with scars, dark spots, skin tags, wrinkles, front lines, excess weight from time to time. I am aging gracefully, and thank God daily.

Ladies, you have to know you are beautiful in God's eyes, and see yourself as that.

There is more than one kind of abuse. Hitting is not the only way to abuse someone. Calling them out of their name, trying to change your appearance, saying you are fat after surgery or after giving birth—it takes a while for your body to regain its shape. Do not allow your spouse or anyone else to degrade you in that way. Know your worth and stand up for yourself.

So much more could be said here—

1. It doesn't matter anymore.
2. Obey God, and you will be okay.
3. Don't let someone make a decision for you and you have to live with it.
4. Change.
5. The Word of God works.
6. Unconditional love.
7. What are you talking about God?
8. This is what I believe:

Hide me behind your thoughts. When you are under God's authority, you know how to operate.

TIME WELL SPENT

A Prayer—

> *Oh, Lord, let thy river flow through thy garden once again.*
> *Let your word work. Be it unto me according to your word. Every word God speaks has its own power to fulfill itself. Bring me where I need to be.*
> *In Jesus's name.*

I prayed that prayer a long time, and to this day, I pray it. It doesn't matter anymore the things that come up on me—your Word is foremost in my life.

"For as much then as Christ hath suffered for us in the flesh, arm yourself with the same mind; for he that hath suffered in the flesh hath ceased from sin." That he is no longer concerned of the fiercer trial, that he no longer should live the rest of his time in the flesh to the lusts of me, but to the will of God. (1 Peter 4:1–2).

Fiery trials are to make you, mold you, conform you to Christ, to take out what does not belong, and Christ formed in you. It is a heart thing. Change your heart.

God is always correct in his acts, ways, plans, or thoughts.

My mind and flesh could not grasp the shaking of a thirty-year marriage. The enemy was given permission to touch it, allowing the hedge of protection to come down, and I could hear, "Have you considered my servant, Lula?"

If it had not been for God's grace and his mercy, I would not have made it through. I give God all the glory for allowing me to partake of sufferings, embracing trials— the end result are wonderful.

Serve God willingly. Don't put anyone or anything ahead of Jesus. Keep him centered in your life, the head of your life.

Mortal man will forsake you, leave you, mistreat, curse out your name, let you down, commit any manner of sin against a marriage—marriage is for ministry!

I heard, "He has sinned against me and me only. You have wounded pride, and your heart is hardened toward him. You must get before me. Seek my face. Seek forgiveness for yourself and against him."

That was hard for a while. My will was in the way. I wanted to get a gun shoot to kill and tell God he died. I am the only one. I know y'all are saints and don't have evil imagination—I was and am real. That's all I know to be. I speak to my poppa as I speak to you.

I am real with everything.

I stayed before God and prayed, and my heart was still hardened. It seemed divorce was inevitable. The divorce came, signed, sealed, delivered. I was set free. I lived a saved, sanctified life unto the Lord and still am now.

I thank God for that life and am forever grateful to him for the kindness he has bestowed on me, and I am not offended in him!

My children—Monsanto, Chauncy, Don—visited him in the hospital on his deathbed.

I led him back to the Lord, prayed with him, and he married his concubine while in the hospital two weeks later. One day after his birthday, he died not my husband.

You kind of grieve quickly with all that's going on.

Don't call or email me with anything. It's not your call. It's because of the hardening of my heart.

Divorce is the result of the hardness of man's heart, but from the beginning, divorce was never part of Gods plan (Matthew 19:8). God likens marriage to the relationship between Christ and the church (Ephesians 5:32)—a union built upon a mutually faithful, endless love for all eternity.

That is the perfection of God. But since the fall of mankind, there are so many things that from the beginning were not so.

It is through Christ's death on the cross, his blood shed for sin, do we find forgiveness for our hardened hearts, and only in the resurrection of Christ can we find power to love in a way that we can withstand any offense and/or betrayal. I learned that and was eventually set free and delivered.

If you stayed and your marriage was put back together, I salute you.

It takes a lot of work, love, trust, communication, lots of prayer. It takes two with Jesus—that middle cord is not easily broken. "Marriage is honorable among all, and the bed undefined; but fornicators and adulterers God will judge" (Hebrews 13:4). I am leaving that right there!

I was beaten unmercifully, and I chose to forgive, and some southerners say, "Treat yourself with a long-handled spoon, forgive, stay away." I did my best to, protect myself from the enemy in him and his friends. It takes two. I could not by myself do anything.

I helped him with the classes, dropped him off, went back an hour later to pick up—no husband. This happened a lot until, one day, I stopped.

My heart was a red color I have ever seen, and around the left and bottom part was a grayish white, stone color, and it dripped of blood slowly. I hurt so badly that I could feel the blood dripping.

If I sat quietly, I could hear the drip. I could not understand why my husband chose his pain and didn't want Jesus. He had witnessed the goodness of God by witnessing many spiritual things after the horrible accident at the plant he worked at, as a construction worker. He had fallen through a hole in the ground, ended up with his back vertebra and ribs broken.

After, the doctors did surgery. It was successful. He was walking but in much pain. The doctors sent him home with a portal in his arm to put medicine (morphine) in his body to help stop the pain. The medicine was delivered at our home. I asked why the medicine was delivered to our home. I was told it was for pain management.

He became a user of street drugs. I watched my husband turn into an addict and becoming a thief, a liar, an emotionally and verbal abuser, not coming home for weeks at a time, and when he did come home, he smelled like cheap perfume and a hole in the wall alley club. I had to throw his clothes away in the trash. It was awful smell. I could not understand until one day, while he was away on his drug, AWOL, I passed near the laundry mat. I was going to visit a lady who had given her life to the Lord. I was checking on her. As I passed by, I heard her voice. I am in here, and I turned inside the laundry mat or washateria.

I was not a laundry mat user. I had a stackable washer and dryer in our home. We prayed and talked awhile, then as I was walking out, I stopped to read the sign on the bulletin board.

It read "Cocaine is my name. I will make you feel good also. I will make you leave your home, your wife, your husband, your children, lose your job and friends. You will steal, kill for me. I am going to lead you down a rugged path. You love me and want me."

I was not used to being around drugs or people that used drugs. My dad was a good policeman. We didn't do that. We were not better than anyone. We stayed home because Dad had enemies, and we could get hurt. He was not playing at all. He carried a gun in his boots, one on his hip, one under his car seat, one in the house. If you looked at it, we were in trouble. He taught us to shoot a rifle and a gun, shooting at cans placed on a post in the field.

I stopped reading. I said, "That's what he is on that drug." My spiritual man jumped inside, and I walked away, went inside my home, and cried as a baby. Fear tried to take hold, but I rose up, praying and rebuking fear, the devil, anything that was moving was under my feet. When he came home, I was not home. I was at the food pantry, volunteering.

When I came home, I opened the door. I smelled sulfur odor. I walked in and heard a bang, as if something had fallen to the ground. I opened the bathroom door. It was my husband with a rubber band around his arm and a needle stuck in his arm. He had fallen in the bathtub. The curtain and rod were down on top of him. He passed out. I tried to pick him up, and he tried to get up but not able to.

I called my friend and asked if our son could stay overnight. I would come for him in the evening. I told her what was happening.

Well, in the middle of the night, he woke up. I asked what happened. The lying began. He had fallen and hit his head.

I said, "But what about the syringe and needle?"

His response was, "What needle?" and started yelling that he needed his money.

I said, "I don't know where you are going, but you are getting out of here. I will call the police, and don't even try taking the car or our son's truck." He was in the marines and left his truck with us.

God caused him to leave without a fight. I had gone to Mr. Billy's office to tell him my husband did not need to borrow against his settlement anymore. He had borrowed over $35,000 and none in the home. The papers were signed, and the borrowing stopped.

He stayed away for months in the street, under the bridges, across the railroad tracks, seen with every race of females and males, lived in buildings with no plumbing or windows, trash everywhere.

How did I know? I went to look for him, and some of our friends knew where he was but could not reach him to get help. I was protecting our son and myself. I found a house, and we moved on Richard Street in Lake Charles.

I allowed him to come home. He was doing better. He had gotten in a rehab class on Fifth Street. We had deposited the checks for me and for him. All was coming together. I was still attending church. Our son was back from the marines, living in his apartment. Our daughter had graduated from UL. Our son was a freshman in high school.

Then one day, he didn't come home after buying a big, white truck and with $20,000 taken out of the account. I went to the bank after three weeks gone, and $5,000 was taken out every week, sometimes more.

Three days later, he returned home and walked in cursing, swinging his fist toward me. Our daughter was visiting at that time.

I was beaten unmercifully with a knife sharpener. He used the big end to hit me repeatedly on my head, just the top as my head was in a grip in the folds of his arm being hit over and over again. Blood was everywhere.

Our daughter tried to stop him from hitting me. As she caught his hand, the knife sharpener hit her face, and blood came out. That was when he stopped hitting me, and I fell to the floor. Our son Chauncy, the marine, came in, and they started arguing. He went to his truck to get something. It was the stick police use to stop people with forcefully. That didn't work. He ended up being cut on his wrist. They had called the police, and my husband was sitting on the steps with his legs crossed as if he had not done anything.

God healed Monsanto as she sang during a church service. Thank God her eyes' scar may be there now.

I had blood coming out of my body out of every opening I have. There was blood in my eyes, ears, mouth, vagina, and rectum, every opening, and the top of my head. My clothes were ripped open. My undergarments where ripped—my breast in full view. The police thought it was our son who had done this. The guns were pointed at him, telling him to get to the ground.

I ran outside and stood in front of our son and screamed at the police, telling them it was my husband that did this, not our son. As I was screaming, I could taste my blood. I became weak and the FBI, DEA, and ATF of Lake Charles Police showed up.

My assistant pastor and office staff showed up. They prayed before we were put in the ambulances. It was a big commotion. I made sure my children were okay. A lot of tests were taken on me from head to toe—nothing broken, no bones were broken. I had a concussion, and my eyesight was dim. Everything was black, then gray, then white, then I could see. I was discharged with my children, and we went to a hotel after securing the house and getting our youngest son from my friend's home. I stayed two weeks in the hotel. My sister would pick our son up for school. She made sure he ate, clothes clean and done, and we slept in the hotel until I could function better. I took the pain medication and slept. I don't know who came, but I told our son, "Don't open the door. Just for my sister and your brother and sister."

Let's go find a lot, and we can call Mr. Y to find out if the lot will hold the house."

We looked near the church we attended and near his school. We found one and bought it, and construction began a month later. At this phase, my husband was incarcerated for three years. I had charges against him for domestic violence and warrants for his arrest in other parts of the state.

We enjoyed the house, furniture, children, grandkids, and church family. We had Bible study. One of the assistant pastors led the group.

We had youth night where females brought their daughters, nieces, and we prayed, ate too much. Many had God filled with the Holy Ghost, and many accepted God as their personal savior. Three girls, who were pregnant, stayed at different times until adoption took place. It was not for a long time. It felt good to help and just listen, not giving advice at all but prayer.

It doesn't matter anymore. Your will be done. In Jesus's name.

Jesus is coming!

"Obey them that have the rule over you, and submit yourselves; for they watch for your souls, as they that must give account, that they may do it with joy, and not with grief: for that is unprofitable for you" (Hebrews 13:17).

> But I say unto you, That whosoever is angry with his brother without a cause shall be in danger of the judgment: and whosoever shall say to his brother, Raca, shall be in danger of the council: but whosoever shall say, Thou fool, shall be in danger of hell fire. (Matthew 5:22)

> For if ye forgive men their trespasses, your heavenly Father will also forgive you: But if ye forgive not men their trespasses, neither will your Father forgive your trespasses. (Matthew 6:14–15)

Get in your Bible as he or she reads. Preach the Word of God. You have to be able to rightly divide the Word of God to be able to do this. Do not put your trust in a woman or man, for they will surely leave you or forsake you, but God will never leave you nor forsake you (Hebrews 13:5).

God is not a man that he should lie (Numbers 23:19).

He or she that possesses the fear of the Lord has wisdom. When you fear God, you will still act the same as with people of God or when you are alone but still in God's presence.

You will not fulfill the lust of the flesh, lust of the eye, and the pride of life.

Have you ever lusted at a thing or a man or a woman? You need the Holy Ghost to be able to not fulfill the lust thereof; the power of the Holy Ghost with fire will help you if you want help.

I have been in three different buildings to be in with people who believe as I did at that time.

I used to teach Sunday school, and I was not a believer. The Holy Ghost was tugging on my heart for a long time. As a child, I was baptized in Jesus's name in the river with all of my siblings. Our mom, Eula Mae Moore Lartigue, was a believer—a very humble woman of God, attending church as an usher since she wore white every Sunday and sat with the other women dressed in white clothing.

Just because you can read and expound well does not give you the right to teach Sunday school as I did. I was in error at that time I finally got it right. I became a believer and part of the body of Christ.

That did not last long. Our mom fell asleep in the Lord in her forties, leaving three grown children—Wilbert, Wilton, Leona—and younger children—Marjorie, Joseph, Adie, Donald Ray, Ella and myself. I was fourteen at that time. We were all two years apart. That was some trying times. If it were not for the Lord and our mom's and other's prayer going on, we wouldn't have made it.

We raised ourselves up all together.

Testimony

There was a meeting at the church I sat in, and this speaker came to minister to the congregation. The ministers were asked to sit close to the front so, when the people came to the altar for prayer, we could reach the front quickly. I love to sit in the front row, so I already had a seat.

The speaker looked at me and asked my pastor at that time in Lake Charles, "Do I have full reign?"

I heard him say, "Go ahead."

I stood up and began moving toward him. As I moved, I could feel the presence of God heavily on me. He put his finger on my forehead.

Out of his mouth came these words:

> There is a generational curse over the females of your family. They die in their forties, and it stops now. In Jesus's name. I hear the Lord say, "It is done." By the blood of Jesus, you are the John the Baptist of your family. You will lead many to the Lord. Not only that, but you will be an example to many.
>
> The gift of prophecy and interpretation is upon you, but you will concede to the true prophets—male and female—when in their presence. Your latter days shall be greater than your former days. I hear the Lord say, "It is done, my daughter!"

My thirty-seven-year-old body just crumbled to the carpet when I came to myself. It was only two ladies and one man sitting, watching me. They helped me up, and I got ready after a while to go home. I slept well and felt lighter than before.

The next day, I was given a copy of the tape. Only God knows where it is today. I was able to write down the prophecy.

At that time, I was thirty-seven, my sister was thirty-nine. Today, we are in our seventies. We had one sister fall asleep in the Lord in her sixties. At the prophecy, she was thirty-five.

My mom went asleep in the Lord in her forties, and one of my sisters as well. Our mom, grandmother, great grand mother all died in their 40's as far as I can calculate from relatives.

God is so good!

My mom had all of her children baptized in Jesus's name in a cold river water with tadpoles everywhere before she fell asleep in the Lord!

Mom O. Chauncy's grandmother shared with me as an adult, later in years, some things about my mom, her salvation, and some of her struggles, all of her life. All I remember is that khaki pants and shirt that Mom laundered and starched with a deep crease in the pant's leg.

Testimony

I was in our home, washing dishes, when I heard behind my ear, "Your earthly dad's soul is required of soon. Ask for his house key and go anoint everything. Clean up and speak to him about salvation. I will prepare his heart!"

I asked my pastor at the time, "When you hear the word soon in the spirit, how long does soon mean?"

He replied, "From one day to a year."

I knew I had to get it done quickly. We were planning a trip to California, to my husband's brother's home in the next month.

My husband would cook daily. My dad would come daily. He would eat and watch TV.

I said, "Daddy, I would like your key to your home to start cleaning it and to wash your clothes. I can send your uniforms to the cleaners too."

He said, "Okay, here you go," and handed me a key.

The assignment began. I would go once a week. I would pray in the Holy Ghost and anoint the doors and furniture. One day, just before we were set to fly out, I asked him if I could pray for him. He said yes. I led him through the sinner's prayer, asked him to ask God to forgive him and to save him. He was seventy-five years old at that time. He had a big smile as I laid hands on him, as I was speaking in tongues.

I said, "You are saved now. Jesus is your friend, and he loves you, Daddy."

He said, "That's good."

He got up to leave, and I said, "We will be leaving for California next week. I was going to ask you to watch Donnie, but when you are at the bus stop for crossing the children, Donnie will need someone with him, so we decided to ask Daddy R., my husband's dad."

He said, "Okay, I will check on them."

I said, "You can still come. He can cook, and we have food cooked. Just needs defrosting and heating the food up."

We got our flight and had a beautiful time visiting. That Thursday, we had planned to go to the mountains, at a camp, on Friday and stay the weekend. The house phone rang. It was my sister. Daddy had passed away. He had a heart attack and was in the hospital. That was what I heard, so we got a red-eye flight to get home.

Daddy passed away on March 7, 1990. God be glorified!

It's good to be obedient to the voice of God. It was three months after I was given the assignment. Thank you, Jesus, for your love!

I stated at the beginning that I would write under the unction of the Holy Ghost and all would not be in order. Hope you can stay with it—it's a journey.

My Heart's Experiences of Many!

The year 2004, in July, right after the convocation services, I had a dream—

I was asleep, and a light shone from my spiritual man (my true self) and pointed at my heart. I cannot put a number on the flashlights searching my heart.

Then in the later part of July, the angel of the Lord appeared unto me and took my heart out of my chest and showed it to me, and I heard, "Get it right, according to my Word." My heart was the prettiest red I had ever seen and around the left and right bottom part was a grayish-white stone in color, and it dripped of blood slowly. I hurt so much that I could feel the drip of blood. I didn't know a human being could hurt so much. Then I thought of the cross and Jesus being on it, taking all of those blows for our sins. I took a look, thinking of myself. After a glimpse of the rugged cross, I looked upon for my salvation.

After true repentance with tears, the hand of the angel appeared and squeezed the right side of my heart, and it stopped bleeding; the stony part then turned into the prettiest red. Then Prophetess hand and face appeared and squeezed the left side, and it stopped bleeding. The white part turned the color of the pretty red, then the angel of the Lord and Prophetess placed my heart on the right side of my chest, and I felt light, as I did when I was getting baptized in Jesus's name (Acts 2:38).

Clean your heart of sin. My heart was not shown to men. It's in our bodies, or picture books have shown it to me as a valentine shape. God reaches you where you are—simple things, no fuss, frailest. Your heart is the entry of feelings, and if you do not guard your heart, you may and can get in trouble and die and go down to hell alive and miss heaven.

In guarding your heart, you can deal with adverse situations quickly if you chose to do so. Do not let the sun go down on your wrath. If that person cannot be reached, continue to go before the Lord until the offense is gone from you.

> *Offense*: "annoyance or resentment brought about by a perceived insult to or disregard for oneself or one's standards or principles," "the action of attacking someone or something."

"The discretion of a man deferreth his anger; and it is his glory to pass over a transgression" (Proverbs 19:11).

"Also take heed unto all words that are spoken; lest thou hear thy servant curse thee" (Ecclesiastes 7:21–22).

"A brother offended is harder to win than a strong city: and their contentions are like the bars of a castle" (Proverbs 18:19).

> Then said he unto the disciples, It is impossible but that offenses will come: but woe unto him, through whom they come!
>
> It were better for him that a millstone were hanged about his neck, and he cast into the sea, than that he should offend one of these little ones.

> Take heed to yourselves: If thy brother trespass against thee, rebuke him; and if he repent forgive him.
>
> And sin against thee seven times a day, and seven times a day turn again to thee, staying I repent, thou shall forgive him. That's every time y'all
>
> (Luke 17:1–4)

I will share how I got to sit in the building for fifteen years in Lake Charles.

God filled me with the Holy Ghost with fire in my home. I was compelled by the Spirit of God.

I turned in my books and key to the pastor from the building I sat in. I asked God for direction on where to go. I was in my home on Eighteenth street and in the shower. I heard a hard knock at the door with all of the water running in the bathroom. It was hard enough that I thought something must be wrong. I got out of the shower, kind of dried up, put my thick white robe on, and walked to the door. I peeped through the peephole and saw a man standing there. He had a blue jeans pants, blue chambray shirt, white tennis shoes, and a chambray hat on. He had an olive color complexion. I was not afraid and not concerned.

I penned the door, and he said, "I have a message for you," and handed me a piece of white paper. He turned and walked away.

I didn't say a word. I closed the door after he left and went to the window to see what he was driving. It only took a few seconds to get to the window, and he was nowhere to be seen.

I sat down at the kitchen table and opened the piece of white paper. It had, "Go to this address: 3950 Gerstner Memorial Lake Charles."

I had never heard or known of this building. I fasted two days, just water, and on Sunday, I drove there by myself. I walked in, was greeted at the door, and found a seat in a steel chair. People would come up to me and welcome me and return to their seats. I enjoyed the praise and worship and the Word of God. I was given an envelope to fill out the information. I did and dropped it in the basket passed by men, who went from each row of seats.

I kept going and signed up to, volunteer and cleanup crew. I do not know how many years that went on. Then it was announced that acre of land had been purchased and a building was going to be built—several buildings. There was a ground breaking, and we ended up on East Guathier Road. It was amazing. They taught the Word, and the praise and worship was awesome. They anointed, and the gifts of tongues and interpretation flowed from two or three, and it was awesome. I immediately ended up on the prayer team, getting there an hour earlier to pray, worked at the nursery, headed the phone ministry, taking phone calls and praying. Eventually, I applied for a job there as custodian and worked with three awesome people one man and two ladies. We formed a relationship and worked well together. On Thursdays, I answered the phone. I stayed there for fifteen years, as a tither, an employee, and made good friends with so many saints.

The pastor was awesome, and as for the staff—we were handled well and not disrespected. Our souls were cared for.

One day, the pastor walked up to me in the foyer and said, "May I see you in my office? you can come now and take your full break later."

I joined him in walking toward his office.

He said, "Open door or closed door?"

I replied, "Open door," and he said, "Have a seat," and said, "I had a dream about you last night. I told my wife about it, and we decided I should tell you."

I was just looking at him as if, what was going on? They had been with me through my husband's drug use and prison time and the building of the new house Donnie and I lived in. Donnie had been filled with the Holy Ghost during children's church at ten.

He said, "I saw you, not here but in another building where your daughter is. You resigned from here and moved away, putting your house up for sale. You will learn so much more there. It will not always be great, but you will be able to function as you do in ministry. Seek the Lord, and you will be obedient. How do you feel about that?"

I said, "I am not sure. I visit there on some Thursdays because we do not work here on Fridays. I make it back for our Sunday services."

He said, "Yes, I know. We always pray for safe travels." He said, "Okay, we shall see if it is God's will or not. I'll see you later. Take your full break, okay?"

I said, "Thank you. See you later."

I remember, during one of the visits, I attended a Thursday service and Prophetess came down from the pulpit and walked down the aisle and put her open hand on my chest and said, "You are the tribe of Levi, and the Lord is calling your name. Lou la—that is how he called me when he spoke to me."

Well, I crumbled to the floor, was held up, and sitting with my daughter holding me.

It was summertime, and the carpet was burgundy.

I got confirmation and resigned that November, found an apartment, found a realtor, and put the house up for sale. Donnie was in college in Baton Rouge, doing well in his studies. His graduation was awesome!

The house sold in nine months. He was in prison for a multitude of things, and he was staying there. I was going on with my life in God.

I made arrangements for an apartment for Donnie, and he lived there for a long time and began opening his shop was an amazing time.

"Vengeance is mine," said the Lord. "I will repay"—

I was a member of a congregation for twenty-four years. I would travel for the last nine years, traveling back and forth to my home, as I was on a journey helping my son with. I would travel over the interstate on Fridays until Sunday after services. Then my son opened another store in Austin, Texas. He asked if I would still help him. He would buy a house after he had secured the building for his second shop. Everything came well together.

On January 1, 2016, I moved in with my son and Sai, still traveling back and forth for fellowship at church services and seeing my daughter Monsanto and son-in-love Gregory Day.

Donnie would get flights out of New Orleans to Austin for years while we stayed home, getting Sai to school doctor's appointment and life.

His realtor friend showed us many houses, but this particular one we kept going to, to see it again. We started going at nighttime to check it out. We applied anointing oil, and the rest is history. We moved in three months after his application.

I let my apartment in April 2021. I did not re-sign the lease. I had been there since 2012. I enjoyed my place, and it was not hard to let it go. I sold all my furniture and donated my clothes.

January 1, 2021—I was awaken by God, and I had pressure at the center of my back. This was one way he used to talk to me or to get something he wants done. I sought the Lord, pulled a few days in partial fasting—just water. I could not get an understanding of what to do.

January 26, 2021—I heard behind my right ear, "Come out."

I said out loudly "God, what do you mean?

> *Rage*: "uncontrollable anger, also known as *wrath,* is an intense emotional state involving a strong uncomfortable and noncooperative response to a perceived provocation, hurt or threat—our emotions are in full force—"
>
> A person in a state of rage may also lose much of their capacity for rational thought and reasoning and may act usually violently on their impulses to the point that they may attack until they themselves have been incapacitated if the source of rage has been destroyed. A person in rage may also experience tunnel vision, muffled hearing, increased heart rate, and hyperventilation.

> Their vision may become rose-tinted, seeing red. They often focus only on the source of their anger. (Wikipedia.org)

I am working on it, constantly casting down thoughts and imaginations! I thank my poppa for helping me! I feel him close with the anointing.

In guarding your heart, you deal with adverse situations quickly.

If you feel offended, let the other party know you feel offended, according to the Word of God. Please do not do as I wanted to do—that would have ended with two deranged people, and that never ends well.

"And because iniquity shall abound the love of many shall wax cold" (Matthew 24:12).

God is not a respecter of persons, even if I think he loves me more than you—no scripture for that one that is the way I feel.

I told you earlier that this is not in any order. I move on to other things!

I chose to read my Bible, pray in the heavenly language God gave me, and stay home—.

"Every day they continued to meet together in the temple court. They broke bread in their homes and ate together with glad and sincere hearts" (Act 2:46).

"Not forsaking the assembling of ourselves together, as the manner of some is; but exhorting one another: and so much the more, as he see the day approaching" (Hebrews 10:25–31).

True Testimony!

> And he shall spread forth his hands in the midst of them, as he that swimmeth spreadeth forth his hands to swim: and he shall bring down their pride together with the spoils of their hands. (Isaiah 25:11)

Chauncy called one day. He said, "Mommy, I have to, pass this swimming test. I am so nervous. All that water with full military gear on my body—what am I gonna do? Hope those few lessons at the YMCA helps."

I said, "I am sure it will, but hold on."

I opened my King James Bible to the back and looked up *swim*. It came up with Isaiah 25:11. I read it and said, "Repeat it after me."

After we finished, he said, "Thank God."

I said, "Do it. Call, give a praise report!"

Well, he called.

He said, "Mom, I passed with flying numbers—one hundred percent."

"Thank you, Jesus," I said.

"Okay, Mommy. I'll call you again."

That's crazy faith.

That is the Word of the Lord for me and everyone else.

God gave me this scripture!

The Spirit of God impressed upon me after hearing this:

"For God is not unjust so as to overlook your work and the love you have demonstrated for his name by having served and continuing to serve the holy ones" (Hebrews 6:10).

I am settled in that.

Resurrection

There will be a resurrection of all dead—both asleep in Christ and the dead, both just and unjust—when the thousand years are finished. The dead will be summoned before the great white throne and their final judgment, and those whose names are not found in the book of life will be cast into the lake of fire forever.

I didn't say that. Read your Bible. Revelation 20:11–15 and John 5:28–29.

Final Judgment

"For we must all appear before the judgment seat of Christ, that everyone may receive the things done in his body, according to that he hath done, whether good or bad" (2 Corinthians 5:10).

> The eternal destiny of every soul shall be meted out by a just God who knows the secrets of the hearts of all men. And before Him shall be gathered all nations; and He shall separate them one from another, as a Shepherd divide his sheep from the goats; and He shall set the sheep on his right hand, but the goats; on the left.
>
> Then shall the King say to them on the right hand, Come he blessed of my Father inherit the kingdom prepared for you from the foundation of the world. Then shall He also say unto them on the left hand, depart from me, be cursed into everlasting fire. prepared for the devil and his angels; and these shall go away into everlasting punishment; but the righteous into life eternal.
>
> (Matthew 25:32–34, 41, 46)

LULA LATIGUE

A True Testimony

The Testimony of the Airport

The marine personnel had picked up Chauncy. He was on his way to California.

I was missing my son so much until I told my husband I have to call him to hear his voice before he leaves. He was supposed to be at the airport soon, according to what we were told.

My husband said, "Lady, you can't call him at the airport."

I said, "Yes, I can. God will do it. Let's go to Kroger store and send a money order to him to have extra money and I can call him."

My husband was shaking his head as we walked to the car. We got to the store and went to the information counter. I asked for a $100 money order and gave the information to the lady. I asked for $5 in quarters. The lady said it came in $10 rolls. I kept giving her money, and I knew I had $105 after the transaction.

I said, "May I borrow the phone book?"

She said I could not, but there was one at the phone booth outside.

I asked to borrow a pen. I said thank-you and walked outside to the phone booth. I do not remember putting any coins in. I asked the operator for the Los Angeles Airport phone number. I wrote the number on the inside of my left hand (husband still shaking his head). I heard the voice saying, "Please deposit $2.50 for the next (I forgot how many minutes). After I deposited the money, I heard the phone ringing. It rang seven times, then I heard a *click*, and I said, "Chauncy."

He said, "Mommy,"

We talked awhile.

I said, "There is a one hundred dollar Western Union check for you.

He said, "Okay, Mommy. I saw one across the way. I will go get it."

I put the phone so my husband could hear Chauncy's voice. His eyes were so big.

"Bye, we'll talk later. I have to get to the gate. I was drawn to the phone booth and answered the phone in here. So many phones, but only this one was ringing. Mommy, I love you."

By this time, I was crying snot everywhere, and my husband was crying too. Tears were just falling! Happy tears for all.

All this for a yearning of a mother's heart to hear her son's voice.

Ain't nothing too hard for God (Genesis 18:14, Jeremiah 32:17).

Who rents a car and drives to Washington, D.C., to visit their son to watch him get medals?

Chauncy's mom, dad, brother—that's who.

We drove from Ville Platte, Louisiana, to see Chauncy guard the military base, but something was wrong on every level with my husband. He drove fast at times and stopped a lot to use the bathroom. When he returned, he was calmer, and it had a scent I could not identify! (Put that, as I call it, in the back of my head.)

We enjoyed Chauncy and went to the beach area in Arlington and sat in a Maserati automobile.

The salesman said, "It takes thirty heads of cattle skin to construct the dashboard."

Chauncy said, "I am buying you one, Mommy, just watch!"

If I told you all that we did while there, it would be a long time of writing, but I will say this—looking at the notes, I did not write down where we stayed.

I have this one written down: My husband turned down a one-way street just to see Chauncy stand at attention near the entrance of the gate.

We walked down the area where the cherry blossoms were in full bloom. It smelled so good. We walked up to the area where Lincoln statute is. There was a presence there—God's presence. I was not sure but I felt a warmth as if in prayer. Perhaps God was getting me ready for the journey that would take place after we returned.

Mr. Chauncy Marcellus Latigue went asleep in the Lord on September 19, 2021, after a forty-three-day—hope this number is correct—battle with COVID. He was not feeling well when he went to get his vaccine. He tested positive for COVID. He did his first works over again—baptism in Jesus's name, refilling of the Holy Ghost after repenting and forgiving all things. Then he was put in an induced coma and ventilator. His vital signs would go up for days and then really low.

When we tested to see if he was fully sedated, his eyebrow raised four times instead of two, so he was given more medicine to fully sedate him.

His birthday was September 12. He was fifty-two years old. Chauncy went asleep on September 19. He was given full marine military honors, and his body was laid to rest on September 24 at the veterans cemetery grounds.

Amazing journey—he loved God, parents, siblings, children, wife, uncles and cousins, his country, his church family, and all of his family members. He never met a stranger.

I salute you, Kenya Najer Couriville Latigue, for taking care of my boy and being a true wife to him as priest of y'all home. May God's peace and supernatural healing take place in your life now and forever!

We thank God for how he took care of Mr. Chauncy while on this earth. He ministered to many through song scripture.

He would tell me, "It seems I can reach others but not my family."

I replied, "Son, there is a time for everyone to get serious about Jesus and accept his death, burial, resurrection as we have. We will keep praying and loving unconditionally."

He quoted scripture at a drop of a hat and loved and lived the Word. He had above-beyond work ethics for every company he worked with.

His job as engineer for Lake Charles was a miracle. He parked on the grounds, pray, and go to work at security job. He did this for seven days, then on the seventh day, he went in and applied. He was hired on the spot.

He called me Lulit. God did it for me. He always wanted to drive the train, and he did until he became ill. The company held his job until they received a call about his passing.

Chauncy left so many little telltale signs. It's as if he knew but could not say.

I made a text including all my nieces, nephews and would give information about their cousin. Those men and women would pray and use scripture and believed all the way that Chauncy was walking out of that hospital healed and whole. I am so proud of them.

Our faith was on trial then and still on trial before God, as Job did. We never gave up nor fainted. We just kept saying, "Until the end," when I received the call from the doctor and Kenya, asking if we wanted the dignity of his passing by naturally letting him go or use the compression and machine.

After the details were given, it was dignity! I was 800 plus miles away. We prayed as they were en route, and when they arrived. They were met at the hospital door and were told that Mr. Chauncy had passed at 1:00 p.m.

After, they were notified by text that "Mr. Chauncy just passed." It was no texting for a minute, but they rose up, comforting themselves and their family. To God be the glory!

> Our time on earth is brief, the number of our days is already decided by you. Every man has been allotted a number of days here on earth. (Job 14:5)

> All the days ordained for me were written in your book before one of them came to be. (Psalm 139:16)

> Whereas ye know not what shall be on the morrow. For what is your life? It is even a vapour, that appeareth for a little time, then vanisheth away. (James 4:14)

> But understand this, that in the last days there will come times of difficulty. For people will be lovers of self, lovers of money, proud, arrogant, abusive, disobedient to their parents, ungrateful, unholy, heartless, unappeasable, slanderous, without self-control, brutal, not loving good, lovers of pleasure rather than lovers of God, having the appearance of godliness, but denying its power. Avoid such people. (2 Timothy 3:1–5)

Donavon Rainey Alfred, March 15, 1975, at three months to a miscarriage. I was at home, and my stomach started hurting. I sat on the commode, and my inside felt as if it was gushing out. After the pain, I got up and a blob and a lot of blood was in the commode. I straightened up and reached inside the commode, picked up the tissue, and put the tissue in a bag, drove myself to the hospital, told them how it happened, and they took the remains and asked if I wanted to donate to science research. In a daze, I agreed. The attendant asked if I had someone to call.

I said, "Yes, my husband."

He arrived an hour later, from work to the hospital, and was very caring and loving. We were discharged after having a dilation and curettage (D&C). We went home. His supervisor drove him and gave him days off.

He cooked, and I slept.

My sister would help with Monsanto and Chauncy.

March 15, 1976—I went into nine months labor. I called the plant to give a message to my husband's supervisor. I was going to the hospital at St. Patrick's; I was in labor. I drove myself to the hospital.

When he arrived, I did not know. I was in hard labor, and the contractions would not stop. My belly would move violently and painfully. I kept going in and out of consciousness. I could not see most of the time and didn't know where I was. There were bright lights and no sound. Then a lady appeared with an outfit of a nun, wearing the whole outfit hat too. She was praying, but I could not hear the words. Then I would here the Our Father prayer but didn't see her but just the words. Then I heard a faint cry, and I passed out. I thought it was three days later, I was awaken and asking for my baby. I screamed so loudly. My husband held me. The nurse gave me a shot to calm me. It was a very sad time leaving the hospital twice in two years without my baby. Then we got home. The nursery bed was up. The changing table had his brand-new clothes. I passed out. I was put in bed, and we cried most of the night and into the next day. I took pills, which the doctor gave, and slept. Horrible time.

I heard the words for a very long time.

I was in a coma for three days, and Ian had died of a myocardial infarction. My husband had buried him in Ville Platte, next to family members, while I was in a coma. I asked what it was in layman's terms.

My husband had to drive to Ville Platte with the small casket for infants in our car because there had been an accident, and the hearse was needed to transport bodies. They had the grave site funeral in 1976. I had ordered a headstone for Ian, Donovan, and

Donald. When Chauncy visited the family, he visited the grave site. He told me, "Mom, daddy doesn't have a headstone or my brothers. I asked for the number and ordered flat headstones for all three."

A Heart Attack, a Blockage of Blood Flow to the Heart Muscle!

My doctor was so concerned after discharging me. He gave me orders, after a month at home, to come volunteer at the hospital as a candy stripper—meaning, I would wear an apron style over my clothes and ask patients from room to room what they wanted to eat. Then he suggested I take the hospice classes. I did, and I wanted to get healed, but I kept thinking my baby was with someone else. They had taken him. I voiced that to him, and I was told, "We would not do anything like that. You have to know that."

I finished the class and was taught well. I said, "How will I ever use this?"

This is not a typo:

March, 15,1975, March 15, 1976—on the same month and date one year later.

Donnie was born on September 21, 1977.

I kind of lost touch. I would argue a lot slept and started imagining seeing my son at different ages with other kids at school, the park, wherever I was.

My husband would say, "You need help. People do not take babies."

I missed the funeral, and the enemy was in my head, telling me he had my baby, that I was not sanctified when I was pregnant, and Donovan and Ian were in hell.

I searched scripture for a long time and could only ask God for his mercy. He has mercy on those he wants to have mercy on.

"For he saith to Moses. I will have mercy on whom I will have mercy, and I will have compassion on whom I will have compassion" (Romans 9:15).

This was in the nineties. I have since come to grips with I cannot take anyone out of hell or put anyone in heaven. It is up to God. I have settled that inside and received God's peace.

"According as he hath chosen us in him before the foundation of the world, that we should be holy and without blame before him in love" (Ephesians 1:4).

"Before I formed thee in the belly I knew thee; and before thou camest forth out of the womb I sanctified thee" (Jeremiah 1:5).

"Seeing his days are determined, the number of his months are with thee, thou hast appointed his bounds" (Job 14:5).

Psalms 139, Psalms 90:1–2, Genesis 2:7, Job 7:1, Job 14:14, Ecclesiastes 3:2.

Just a few—it's actually from Genesis to Revelations.

Military Police in San Antonia, Texas
January 16, 1989

We received a letter from the marine department, informing us that Chauncy was being awarded a military police pin award and a marksman pin and the information to attend. My husband and I read the letter, and he said, "We need gas, money, food, and a car."

I said, "In faith, I believe God will provide for us to go there."

The next day, Clearance knocked on the door of our apartment on Eighteenth street. My husband opened the door.

Clearance said, "man you can use my truck to go visit Chauncy. I had the tires rotated and oil changed. Here is one hundred dollar for gas."

I had $50 under the mattress, and we traveled well. We never ran out of money. It just kept manifesting as we traveled, put gas in the truck, and bought food.

I was sitting at the table, reading my Bible. I put the letter on the table and prayed, asking for favor and money to attend the ceremony.

We packed our clothes in two suitcases. We were just smiling and thanked God for providing.

We started our journey—our son Donnie, my husband, and I. When we arrived at the gate, we were given a window ticket and told where we were to stay and were given more information about the ceremony.

Ceremony day— we were led to a building and went down a hall. At the end of the hall, Donnie recognized Chauncy and ran toward him. They hugged, and we all hugged. Chauncy was surprised to see us. I cried softly during the whole time.

We heard a voice instructing us to make our way to an area.

Chauncy said, "I have to go. See y'all in the room."

We were ushered to sit in an area. The program began after a lot of men and women walked in with so many pins on their uniforms. They looked really classy and, I suppose, important to the country.

A person came toward where the parents were seated, and we were informed that when the name of our son or daughter was announced, we should make it to the front and pin the medal on the uniform of our son or daughter.

My husband stood up so fast I didn't get a chance to stand and move forward. He was proud, and it showed. Donnie was taking it all in, just quiet. Then we all gathered for a while in the hall—congratulations and hugging. Then we heard more instructions.

Chauncy said, "I have to go."

We were led to, the outside, toward bleachers, as if at a football game, but it was the pomp and circumstance of the marine band and the men and women marching as they approached the seated area. As they passed in front of the bleachers, the men and women's head turned toward us. It was amazing, and that carried power and proudness as if to say I made it.

Then the men and women that were being honored with the pinning ceremony were told to stand.

Chauncy would drive four hours to visit me, just a blessing. We would cook everything he wanted to eat and had a blast on the boat rides and just riding around. He said on his last visit, "Mommy, I am going to move here. I just need to get my honey bunny to agree, and we are coming!"

Signs of His Coming

The days of perils are here, with forms of godliness void of the power of God. Society and politics corrupted men's hearts, filled with pride, blasphemies, unholiness, and love of evil and pleasures (2 Timothy 3:1–13). These things, together with multitudes running to and fro, the increase of knowledge (Daniel 12:4), the traffic of automobiles (Nahum 2:2:3), and the persecution of the Jews and the return of Palestine. Luke 21:24 are startling signs that Jesus's coming draws nigh.

Wars and rumors of wars, famines, earthquake, storms, floods, distress of nations with perplexity, and men's hearts failing them for fear are sounding the alarm that Jesus is coming is at hand (Luke 21:25–28, Matthew 24:6, 11 Timothy 3:1–13, Daniel 17:4, Nahum 2:3, Matthew 24:6, Luke 21:25–28.

Second Coming of Christ

Jesus Christ is coming back to earth in bodily form, as he went away (Acts 1:11), to catch away a holy people, his bride, his church, who have accepted redemption through his blood by birth of water and of the spirit and who are found faithful when he comes.

> For the Lord himself shall descend from heaven with a shout, and with the voice of the archangel and with the trump of God; and the dead in Christ shall rise first; then we which are alive and remain shall be caught up together with them in the clouds to meet the Lord in the air; and so shall we ever be with the Lord. (1 Thessalonians 4:16–17)

One shall be taken and the other left (Luke 17:34–36, Acts 3:19–21, 1 Corinthians 11:26, Philippians 3:20–21, Titus 2:13–14).

My God from Zion!

I salute Donnie for upgrades to my life!

It was not in the fruit Eve took a bite of. It was her disobedience, and that spirit got on her husband, and sin set in for us all. The redemption was and still is the cross, the death, the burial, and the resurrection of Jesus.

I believe that the saints of God will *not* be raptured away but will go through the tribulation until such time as God himself will use the earth to remove them and protect them.

Matthew 24:1–31
Ezekiel 7:19
Revelation 14:7
Revelation 15:4
Revelation 16:5
Joel 2:2
Amos 5:18, 20
Isaiah 26:20–21

"And to the woman [the church] were given two wings of a great eagle, that she might fly into the wilderness, into her place, where she is nourished and the Earth helped the woman" (Revelation 12:10–17).

Moreover, I believe that the distress upon the earth is the beginning of sorrows and will become more intense until there shall be a time of trouble such as there never was since there was a nation even to that same time. The body of Christ is being made aware that the beast is the son of perdition and not to take the mark.

Millennium

I believe that period of tribulation will be followed by the dawn of a better day on earth and that, for a thousand years, there shall be peace on earth (Revelation 20:1–5, Isaiah 65:17–25, Matthew 5:5, Daniel 7:27, Micah 4:1–2, Hebrew 2:14, Romans 11:25–27).

Resurrection

There will be a resurrection of all the dead, both just and unjust, when the thousand years is finished. The dead will be summoned before the great white throne for their final judgment, and those whose name is not found in the book of life will be cast into the lake of fire forever (Revelation 20:11–15, John 5:28–29).

Final Judgment

"For we must all appear before the judgment seat of Christ; that may receive the things done in his body, according to that he hath done, whether good or bad" (2 Corinthians 5:10).

The eternal destiny of every soul shall be metered out by a just God who knows the secrets of the hearts of men.

> And before *him* shall be gathered all nations; and he shall separate them one from another, as a shepherd divide the sheep from the goats; and he shall set the sheep on his right hand, but the goats on the left.
>
> Then shall the king say to them on the right hand, Come he blessed of my father inherit the kingdom prepared for you from the foundation of the world. Then shall he also say unto them on the left hand, Depart from me, ye cursed, into everlasting fire, prepared for the devil and his angels; and these shall go away into everlasting punishment, but the righteous into life eternal (Matthew 25:32–34, 41, 46)

To my daughter, Mrs. Monsanto Chloe' Day, you have been and still are a blessing to me in so many ways. Most of all, with your prayers reaching heaven for me. While God was visiting you in our homes—I says *homes* because we moved a lot for so many reasons—you prayed in every one of the homes as a child. I remember your visitation from the Holy Ghost in the building in Ville Platte, your aunt bringing you home all wet, dripping of water and you had not been in water but God had visited you at seven years old.

I changed your clothes and put you in your bed. You slept through the night with a glow all over you. I bless the name of Jesus for that and many other times of his presence in our home. When you prayed, the spirit of God would appear from under the door and just hover near the door, descending and ascending on the door—a sweet rose fragrance would come with that. Amazing of God to visit us. Finally the transformation began and salvation set in.

All of the times you were in college and your visits. I am grateful for all. It was preparing me for war against the enemy with the situation of choices my husband began to make.

Monsanto Chloe' Day—a heavy calling on your life with a mantle sent and given by God. I am proud of who you have become and are becoming, not perfect but still being blessed by God in every way, loving God's people and ready to help. Remember, you are not a doormat to be used by takers, keep them far away, and God has never rejected you in life. He has always carried you through many waters, but you never drowned. I salute you in Jesus's name! The gifts are not for you, the gifts are for the people! But don't let people use the gifts placed inside of you for their gain.

Mr. Donnie Alfred—you are quiet a soft-spoken, humble hard worker and a saved man of God. It's been a journey with you and helping and watching you blossom in every area of your life. Very quiet, but don't let people use you for their gain as well. You are a kind, loving man.

God said, "What is happening in your life now, I will not write it here." But you know what he said about you? Hold fast to him, pray daily, use your business as a platform to minister to people. You don't need a pulpit setting to tell of the goodness of God. Perhaps you can tell your testimony when a building comes up for ministry for our family, you can share as a man of God, living the good life as a believer in Christ.

God has allowed you to accomplish all you have today, including getting filled with the Holy Ghost at ten years old, speaking in other tongues. The judge's daughter prayed for you and, after children's church, she ran up to me in the hall, all excited and getting baptized in Jesus's name as an adult.

I thank God for you upgrading my life, protecting us and being a blessing.

I never imagined my life this way. I am humbled and grateful!

Keep the takers, fakers away.

To my grandchildren at this writing,

Some of you were born in a saved house—meaning, you were raised in God wherever your parents were in their relationship with him. Some may not be, but you are in the family now and glad you serve our God. Every one of you have a calling on your life and are given spiritual gifts and natural gifts. Seek God for help, ask for wisdom. He will give it freely. Y'all stay saved. Pray up, so when crisis comes, you will not faint.

Get off social media, read your Bible. That is what is needed—your face in the Bible, not on FaceTime or Facebook, airing all your business to the world, letting people talk. They do not have it all together. All you have is your family.

You are going to look for some family with a flashlight in the daytime—that is an old saying.

That means old school—when you keep pushing your family away and not keeping in contact with them, it will not be good in the future. Your dad's and mom's people are family—get in contact with them.

Y'all can start a text with cousins and pray for each other, not telling each other off that one is better than others. All have gifts, money, and some use it wisely while some waste it. Upgrade your life. Family is all you have. Stay saved. Repent often. Forgive quickly. Every one of you go through some more than others, but all can help out. Your family is all you have. Fix the part you messed up and live according to the Word of God. Be a leader. Profess Jesus openly and work hard. Let your silence be heard after you reach your goals. Save your money, buy wisely, prepare for the tribulation, store up stuff for later. Make sure everyone has food, water, etc.

I love y'all. I speak a blessing over y'all of the legacy of *faith in God's Word*!

Don't buckle, praise him instead.

My great grandchildren,

The Lord protect y'all in Jesus's name!

All have gifts and praying for y'all daily. The half has not been told of your journey!

Keep the faith in God. So happy you're my great-grand however the circumstances.

Well, I will keep writing, expecting God to move as he said about the books I pen!

Keep the faith in God.

"Marvel not that I said unto thee, You must be born again" (John 3:7).

Father, I confess my sins to you only, and I ask you to forgive me of every sin I have committed against you and you only. I repent of everything. Bring to my thoughts what I have forgotten my childhood sin, my teenage sin, and my adult sin. Help me, Lord Jesus. I confess Jesus as my personal Savior, and help me live for you fill me with your precious Holy Ghost so I can have my own prayer language to talk with you. I want to live for you until my time is done on this Earth. My soul loves you, Jesus. Help me overcome my flesh. Show me where I can sit in a building with a congregation that can help me walk with you. I thank you, Jesus, for your love. I believe you died on the cross for me, and I thank you. I am saved and safe in your love.

End

ABOUT THE AUTHOR

Lula Maude Latigue was born in the country in Vidrine, Louisiana. She attended and graduated from Joseph Celestine High School in Mamou, Louisiana, and graduated salutatorian of her class of six students in 1966. She received a business scholarship to Dallas Business Institute but did not complete the college courses. Lula is a mom to five children. A mother in Israel to many.

Lula's close circle of friends thinks she is awesome. She has a sense of humor and eats dessert on too many occasions. She loves unconditionally and has to think before she speaks because she is a disciplinarian from childhood. Lula loves the Lord Jesus. Her testimonies are true.

Lula is a Christian who believes in the death, burial, resurrection of Jesus Christ and is water baptized in Jesus's name. God filled her with his precious Holy Ghost. She speaks in other tongues and believes Jesus is coming back for his church of saints.

Lula is a spoiled mom. Her children love her and want to be around her, as do her grandchildren. It's a pleasure to serve God and his people of humanity. She finds it a blessing to be part of Christendom and experience the anointing and peace only God can give. She lives in Texas, a transplant from Vidrine, Mamou, Lake Charles, Abbeville. Jesus is coming back!

Are you ready?

www.ingramcontent.com/pod-product-compliance
Lightning Source LLC
LaVergne TN
LVHW060831080125
800786LV00009B/52